Supporting parents and carers

A trainer's guide to positive behaviour strategies

Sharon Paley, Chris Stirling and Mark Wakefield

British Library Cataloguing in Publication Data

A CIP record for this book is available from the Public Library

© BILD Publications 2008

BILD Publications is the imprint of:
British Institute of Learning Disabilities
Campion House
Green Street
Kidderminster
Worcestershire DY10 1JL

Telephone: 01562 723010
Fax: 01562 723029
E-mail: enquiries@bild.org.uk
Website: www.bild.org.uk

ISBN 978 1 905218 07 3

BILD Publications are distributed by:
BookSource
50 Cambuslang Road
Cambuslang
Glasgow G32 8NB

Telephone: 0845 370 0067
Fax: 0845 370 0064

For a publications catalogue with details of all BILD books and journals telephone 01562 723010, e-mail enquiries@bild.org.uk or visit the BILD website www.bild.org.uk

Printed in the UK by Latimer Trend & Company Ltd, Plymouth

Illustrations by Eleanor Ward

The British Institute of Learning Disabilities is committed to improving the quality of life for people with a learning disability by involving them and their families in all aspects of our work, working with government and public bodies to achieve full citizenship, undertaking beneficial research and development projects and helping service providers to develop and share good practice.

We are grateful to Positive Options for their help in the development of this publication.

Contents

4

Introduction

Parents and carers are often the most important influence on a child's life. They are there for most of the child's formative years and build up important relationships. And yet they very rarely receive training strategies to help them deal with challenging behaviour. Some have their own views and strategies and are able to provide important insight into the whys and wherefores of their child. Others will find it reassuring to be trained by people who are in, or have been in, the same situation as themselves. They are likely to respond more positively from peer training and so gain more from it.

It would be useful for trainers to try and identify from initial sessions those participants who may be willing and able to deliver the training themselves, either on their own or in conjunction with another professional, at least in the first instance. Alternatively, organisations that wish to deliver this training could be encouraged to recruit parents and carers who are interested in attending a 'training the trainer' session to assess their abilities and skills.

Although the importance of including parent and carer trainers is acknowledged, it should be recognised that a professional trainer may need to play a role at the beginning to offer support and guidance as well as to ensure quality.

Trainers should use these session plans when delivering the theoretical component of the training to a group of parents and carers. The course content is designed to be easily understood by parents and carers who may have limited previous formal training, and trainers should always assess the individual needs of the people participating in any course they are undertaking.

Session plan times are given in the margin and are approximate only but the course is designed to be completed in under six hours.

Session 1
Introducing the course

Materials needed

PowerPoint projector and screen

Handout 1

flipchart paper and pens

paper and pencils

3–4 boxes with junk, glitter, art and craft material, Sellotape and glue

> **PowerPoint Slides 1–4**
>
> The aim of this session is to make participants feel comfortable with the training course.

If the venue is unfamiliar, cover the domestic arrangements such as fire exit details and where the toilets are located. Explain when breaks will occur.

 Distribute Handout 1 and ask participants if they have any questions.

 Show PowerPoint Slides 1–2. These give course and session titles.

Show PowerPoint Slide 3. Make sure that all participants understand the aims and objectives of the course.

 Show PowerPoint Slide 4. It is important to set a joint agenda and engage the participants in the ground rules. Check if participants would like to add to them and explain that they can add or remove rules during the course.

Introduce Activity 1 to help remove barriers and allow participants who may not be familiar with one another to start talking.

Activity 1

Breaking the ice

Select one or more of the following ice-breakers, making sure that you adjust the total time required for the session accordingly. If more than one ice-breaker is used participants need only introduce themselves once.

Ice-breaker 1

Ask participants to form small groups of 2–4 people, introduce themselves to the others in their group and together give three reasons they are undertaking the training. Allow a few minutes for this and then ask each group to choose an individual who will feed back to the whole group on their behalf. Record the results on a flipchart so that you can refer to points raised as they are dealt with throughout the training.

Ice-breaker 2

Ask each participant to take a piece of paper and draw a line to divide it in two. Ask them to make a drawing which best represents them as a person on one half and on the other a drawing of an unfulfilled ambition. Ask everyone in turn to introduce themselves, show the drawings to the group and explain what they represent. Stress that this Activity is not about artistic ability!

Ice-breaker 3

Prepare 3–4 boxes with junk, glitter, art and craft material, Sellotape and glue. Wrap the boxes or close them tightly. Divide participants into groups of 2–4 people and ask them to open the boxes and make an animal, vegetable or mineral representation from the contents of the box. When they have finished, ask them to introduce themselves and their craft work to the whole group.

Session 2
Defining challenging behaviour

Materials needed

PowerPoint projector and screen

Handout 2

flipchart paper and pens

> **PowerPoint Slides 5–14**
>
> The aim of this session is to define challenging behaviour and describe its characteristics.

5 ▶ **Show PowerPoint Slide 5** to introduce the session. We all have a different values base and this will affect what we feel is acceptable behaviour and how we react to it. Swearing is the most unacceptable thing some people can think of but it may have no impact on others at all. We want to look at what we individually find challenging and difficult. It will be useful if participants give examples of what they find challenging. This will allow them to see that those giving the training are, or have been, in the same position as themselves and will build empathy and rapport. Point out that challenging behaviour is not necessarily all about physical and verbal aggression or general acting out. It covers a range of behaviours, including passive behaviour and self-harming. However, we also need to recognise that in some circumstances professional help may be useful or necessary.

6 ▶ **Show PowerPoint Slide 6** and **introduce Activity 2.** This Activity will enable participants to examine the difference between their feelings about behaviour and what a behaviour is.

Activity 2

What makes a behaviour challenging to you?

Split the participants into groups of 2–4 people and ask them to think about the behaviours they are experiencing and what aspects of the behaviours they find challenging. Give them a few moments to think about this and write these down on paper provided. Now ask them to discuss with the person next to them why they find some behaviour difficult.

Ask those who feel happy to do so to tell the whole group. Compare answers people give and discuss how personal experience, mood and capacity to manage a behaviour can affect our view of some behaviours. It may also be useful to ask about different situations, for example family gatherings or shopping trips, and how these can alter the way the behaviour is perceived.

Use the feedback from the exercise to show the difference between a 'behaviour' and a 'feeling'. It is likely that some participants will confuse the two. Make a list of the challenging behaviours that are being experienced in each group on the flipchart. Ask the other groups if they have experienced any of those identified by each group in turn. It is highly likely that they have, even though they may not have listed them. This will probably lead to further discussion about particular behaviours.

Participants are unlikely to give hard and fast solutions to these problems as one problem may have many solutions, depending on the circumstances. However, in discussing the points they will hopefully pick up tips and strategies that they may be able to employ.

Ask the group if they have found any good ways of dealing with certain problems.

Show PowerPoint Slide 7. Use this Slide to reinforce the outcomes of the exercise and to ensure that participants understand the word 'behaviour'. It may also be useful to make the point that 'naughty' is not a behaviour but a word we use to describe lots of different behaviours we don't like. Explain that it is necessary to be specific about the behaviour so that it can be dealt with effectively.

 Show PowerPoint Slides 8–12. Lead a discussion on the five characteristics of behaviours and encourage participants to give their views on each aspect and how it affects them in individual circumstances. The five characteristics are listed individually below with more detail on each. It is the combination of each of these to a lesser and greater extent that determines how well we will deal with them. For example, if a behaviour happens a lot, lasts for a long time, is considered to be unacceptable by a majority of people, makes us feel very unsure of ourselves and puts us or the child or others at risk then we are likely to find that very difficult to deal with.

Intensity A behaviour may often feel more intense and difficult than it appears to others because of the way it is experienced, the way it makes us feel and the words we use to describe it. The behaviour may have become more noticeable because of its frequency and this in turn may make it appear more intense. Allow participants to give their answers to the words that describe the behaviour.

Frequency It is helpful to know if the behaviour always occurs at the same time or in the same set of circumstances. Carers will be able to better manage a behaviour if they know when it is going to happen. Some behaviours only occur in certain circumstances or when certain factors are present. These are often called 'triggers'. It may be that what appears to be one behaviour is in fact a combination of behaviours, or a series of behaviours where one behaviour triggers another. There may be different behaviours for different situations or one overriding behaviour. If the primary behaviour is identified and sorted out, the development of management strategies may have a beneficial impact on the other related behaviours.

Duration This is important because if the behaviour goes on long enough to achieve the desired effect, it is then strengthened and repeated. It is often this point which parents find most difficult to cope with as giving in becomes the easy option in the short term. To be harassed for a long period is difficult to deal with. The other point is how long the behaviour has been present. If the behaviour began relatively recently (days/weeks) it is likely to be easier to manage than one that has been going on for months or years.

Social acceptability The behaviour will have a reason for being there. It may be being used to elicit interaction with others or gain a specific outcome, for example to gain something desirable or to avoid something unpleasant. It may be something that when done in a different environment would be easy to deal with. Participants should think about how they would normally deal with the behaviour and what it is about the situation that makes it more difficult for them. This may be because of social pressures such as what others are thinking about them in a public place. Encourage the participants to talk about situations in which they have found themselves, explore how they dealt with them and what they may do differently next time. Encourage them to think about having strategies in place before the behaviour occurs so that they know what they are going to do.

Risk In simple terms, risk is the potential for harm that can occur from the behaviour directly. It can be social, psychological or physical. Examples include being unable to participate in social activities such as going to the supermarket; withdrawing social interaction; being hit, bitten or kicked; and placing self or others in danger from the surroundings such as on the street near a busy road or in a room with an open fire. The level of risk to the people experiencing the behaviour will affect how you react/deal with it. Discuss examples from the group.

Show PowerPoint Slide 13. Draw together the information from the previous Slides and go through Slide 13, exploring how it relates to the experience of the participants.

 Show PowerPoint Slide 14 and **introduce Activity 3.** This Activity is intended to promote discussion of issues relating to behaviours that the participants are experiencing or have experienced in the past and that they have found challenging.

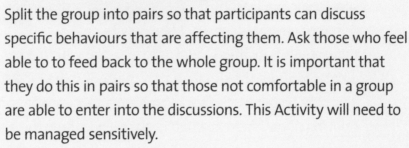

Activity 3

What behaviours are affecting you?

Split the group into pairs so that participants can discuss specific behaviours that are affecting them. Ask those who feel able to to feed back to the whole group. It is important that they do this in pairs so that those not comfortable in a group are able to enter into the discussions. This Activity will need to be managed sensitively.

 Distribute Handout 2 and ask participants to complete it.

Session 3

What causes challenging behaviour?

Materials needed

PowerPoint projector and screen

Handout 3

flipchart paper and pens

PowerPoint Slides 15–22

The aim of this session is to give participants some insight into behaviours and the reasons for them.

15 ▶ **Show PowerPoint Slide 15** to introduce the session. There seems to be no reason for some behaviours and some behaviours may have reasons incorrectly assigned to them.

16–17 ▶ **Show PowerPoint Slides 16–17** and go through each of the personal and environmental factors in turn, indicating how they may cause a particular type of behaviour. Some may not seem relevant to some of the participants. If there are parents of children with learning disabilities some of the reasons may have particular relevance. You may need to give more detail on specific causes of learning disability to illustrate the points.

18 ▶ **Show PowerPoint Slide 18** and **introduce Activity 4.** This Activity will enable participants to identify possible reasons for various different behaviours they have encountered.

Activity 4

Identifying the causes of behaviour

Split the group into groups of 2–4 people and hand out flipchart paper and pens. Tell them to divide their paper down the middle and write 'Personal' at the top of the left-hand column and 'Environmental' at the top of the right-hand column. Ask participants to complete the lists with as many examples as they can think of in their group. Then ask someone to feed back to the whole group. Look for similarities and differences and compare people's views. It may be useful to refer to Activity 2 to bring out other aspects they have already discussed and show how these all link together.

 Show PowerPoint Slides 19–20 which allow participants to identify, or begin to identify, why their child is using behaviour and what it is like.

10
minutes

 Show PowerPoint Slide 21. Explain the ABC of behaviour and what the function of the behaviour is, using the example of an awkward teenager:

10
minutes

Antecedent:	*What causes the behaviour*	John is asked to get up and get dressed
Behaviour:	*What the teenager does*	ignores the request and continues to sleep
Consequences:	*What happens as a result of the behaviour*	John's parents get fed up with asking and withdraw the request

Participants should be made aware that it is not always easy to determine the antecedent, especially in cases where the behaviour has been present for a long time. There may also be biological factors that may cause specific behaviours in individuals but they can be managed with the strategies provided here.

People will not change their behaviour if they do not have a good reason for doing so. For example, it is difficult for most people to stop smoking and they will make excuses for not doing so: 'I'll do it after Christmas', 'I'll just finish this packet', 'I'll get fat if I stop'. However, if they were suddenly diagnosed with a related illness most would try to stop straight away. This is because they now have a good reason to change their behaviour. The same is true for challenging behaviour. The behaviour serves a purpose and until the child finds a way of achieving the same outcome by a different way of behaving they will carry on with the behaviour they are most familiar or comfortable with.

Participants need to find a way of supporting their child to see that doing things a different way can bring the same results. The following positive behaviour management strategies can be used to help participants achieve this.

Allow participants to give examples of their own experiences. They may now be able to see how this has developed. Explain that they must want a change if they are to be successful in replacing undesirable behaviours with new ones.

Show PowerPoint Slide 22 and explain the five outcomes achieved through behaviour:

10 minutes

Communication and interaction:	*where the behaviour is designed to communicate the need for attention*
Sensation:	*where the behaviour itself is stimulating and enjoyable because it makes the child feel good*
Tangible benefit:	*where the child may gain activities or objects they like as a result of the behaviour*
Demand avoidance:	*where the child is rewarded by the removal of a demand as in the previous scenario*
Social avoidance:	*where the child is avoiding a social situation they find difficult*

 Distribute Handout 3 and ask participants to complete it. Discuss answers with the whole group.

15 minutes

Session 4
Relationships and behaviour

Materials needed

PowerPoint projector and screen

Handout 4

> ### PowerPoint Slides 23–27
>
> The aim of this session is to show how we all behave differently in any given situation.

Show PowerPoint Slide 23 to introduce the session. Children will often behave better for other people than they do for their parents. Explain that how we react depends upon who we are dealing with. For example, we talk to a toddler differently from the way we talk to a teenager, a work colleague, a friend or the person who serves us in the supermarket, and differently from our parents. Consequently, the function of behaviour changes with the context. How often do parents say they wish their child treated them the same way they do their grandparents or friends' parents? You could mention Harry Enfield's teenage character Kevin as an example of this.

Show PowerPoint Slide 24. Stress that behaviour is a way of communicating and telling us something. Explain that when we talk to children about their behaviour it is important to be specific about what it is we do and do not like and that we should take the time to point out appropriate behaviour wherever possible. Remind participants that 90 per cent of communication is body language – facial expression, how we stand, tone of voice, etc.

Show PowerPoint Slide 25 and use the example of 'sulking' to illustrate this Slide. If there is no one to see us sulk there is no point in sulking. We tend to sulk in public so that people take notice of us and reward us with attention, and we may even get something tangible, such as what we were sulking for or interaction and communication with others.

 Show PowerPoint Slide 26 which lists some of the things that a person with particularly challenging behaviour may be missing. Challenging behaviour can be the outcome of any of the missing items listed, or a combination of them. There may be others. Missing these items does not, of course, mean that a difficult behaviour will occur. Challenging behaviour is only one way of coping with these problems.

What do we mean by each of the missing items?

Communicating effectively and forming meaningful relationships
People should be valued as individuals and their views taken account of. Typically, these relationships are with parents or carers, other family members and friends and are built on mutual respect and trust, and not on power.

Safety and well-being People need to know that they are safe where they live and that they are being looked after. If these factors change, say through being moved around foster placements, they become anxious and less well looked after no matter that they are being provided with the best possible care. Building up a trusting relationship takes time.

Influence and control People need to have some say in what they do with their lives and not be restricted by too tight regulations.

Meaningful occupation People need to do things that are important and interesting to them. Without this, using behaviour may be a way of reacting to the situation.

Look forward to People need to have something to look forward to. If they feel that what they do has no positive outcome they may resort to challenging behaviour as a way of showing this and trying to change things.

Self-worth People need to have self-esteem or a sense of self as an individual. If they have low self-esteem they will find it difficult to see why they need to change their behaviour. 'It doesn't matter anyway. Whatever I do it's just the same.'

Relevant skills People may need to be given the skills and knowledge to enable them to manage their behaviour. If a behaviour has been present for a long time they may not know how to change, or find change difficult. It is up to us to provide them with these skills.

Supporters If those supporting the child are finding things difficult they are likely to find it hard to keep going without support. This may result in an inconsistency in their approach and lead to the child feeling unsafe because the boundaries are failing. This in turn may lead to an escalation in the difficult behaviour.

Make it clear to participants that in identifying possible reasons for the difficult behaviour they are not being judgemental. Participants need to feel supported by the training. They may recognise that some of the points raised are relevant to themselves. Point out that part of the reason for doing this training is to help them understand the behaviour so that they can go away and try to address the problems as they relate to themselves.

 Show PowerPoint Slide 27. Explain that the pyramid represents the skills, feelings and needs detailed on Slide 26. The more of these that are present the fuller the pyramid will become and therefore the fewer difficult behaviours will present themselves. This is represented by the point of the pyramid. The base, which is wider, represents the greater number of difficult behaviours that are present because of the lower number of skills and needs that are present in the child.

 Distribute Handout 4 and ask participants to complete it. Discuss answers with the whole group.

Session 5
De-escalation and distraction

Materials needed
PowerPoint projector and screen
Handout 5
flipchart paper and pens

> **PowerPoint Slides 28–29**
> The aim of this session is to provide participants with strategies for dealing with challenging behaviour.

28 **Show PowerPoint Slide 28** to introduce the session.

29 **Show PowerPoint Slide 29** and **introduce Activity 5.** This Activity will help participants to identify ways of managing challenging behaviour.

Activity 5
Dealing with challenging behaviour
Ask participants as a group to list ways to de-escalate and distract. Ask them to think about what their child enjoys and if this could be used to advantage.

continued

Use the definitions below to explain the process of dealing with behaviours. Explain what measures can be taken once a situation has developed.

De-escalation is the process of trying to prevent the development of a behaviour that is happening by adopting appropriate measures. The following techniques can help to calm a situation down:

- Use calming body language, stand or sit in a pacifying manner, speak in a calm tone of voice or use a calming touch.

- Explain that it is the behaviour, not the child, that is the problem being dealt with.

- Avoid confrontation when not letting the child engage in their behaviour. Shouting at them will only make the situation worse.

- Remind the child of the consequences of their actions without threatening punishments for behaviour as this may escalate the situation.

- Avoid having an audience by asking the other children or uninvolved adults to leave as this is often easier than trying to move the child who is upset and in crisis.

- Ensure that everyone involved deals with challenging behaviours in a consistent and calm approach because any differential in the approach can lead to the individual concentrating their efforts on the person they see as the most likely to give them what they want.

Distraction is the process of drawing a person's attention away from the cause of a behaviour. The following techniques can help to take the child's mind away from the cause of the challenging behaviour:

 Encourage the child to engage in an activity that they like that will give them something else to do as this will allow them to calm down and move them on from the crisis. It will also give an opportunity to interact positively with them and develop a dialogue.

Offer the child a way out of the confrontation by giving them an option that they will not see as a loss of face and by not backing them into a corner.

Talk to the participants about how to use these techniques, what it might be like for them, what situations they have found themselves in and what has worked for them.

5 **Distribute Handout 5** and ask participants to complete it. Discuss answers with the whole group.

10 minutes

Session 6
Defusion

Materials needed
PowerPoint projector and screen
Handout 6

20 minutes

> **PowerPoint Slides 30–31**
> The aim of this session is to show how to prevent challenging behaviour from happening.

 Show PowerPoint Slide 30 to introduce the session.

 Show PowerPoint Slide 31 and stress that prevention is always better than cure.

Defusion is the process of preventing a crisis by intervening at an early stage. The following techniques can help to prevent challenging behaviour:

- When a challenging behaviour has been dealt with and everything is calm, talk to the child about what happened and why. Give them a strategy for dealing with that particular situation in future and tell them how to react next time.

- Reinforce appropriate behaviours and ignore negative ones, for example by praising a young girl for helping her sister to colour in a picture while ignoring the fact that they snapped the crayons.

- Give positive comments whenever possible as this gives the child a sense of worth, builds their self-esteem and encourages more positive actions, for example saying that the child made a lovely cup of tea even if it wasn't.

Avoid confrontational situations by anticipating possible problem areas and have a strategy ready to deal with those that do arise, for example if being late is a problem telling them that the appointment is half an hour earlier than it really is.

Reward the child for their behaviour, making it clear what they are being rewarded for, and never take the reward away once it has been offered.

Keep the boundaries firm, for example by sticking to a decision once it has been communicated. However, it may be sensible on occasion to negotiate if that may be a way of dealing with a situation better in the future.

Have a set of ground rules that can be referred to to remind the child what is expected of them. Make sure the child knows what the ground rules are and understands them and what the consequences will be for breaking them.

Show the child how to behave by example. Children learn behaviour from those around them, most importantly from their parents.

Tell participants what signs to look out for to stop a situation developing. Just as triggers are different for each child and being aware of these make it easier to prevent behaviour escalating, so the outward signs that a child is stressed, upset or feeling frustrated will also be different. Give them some practical ideas that may be of use to them based on feedback from the group. Stress the importance of using positive behaviour strategies.

 Distribute Handout 6 and ask participants to complete it. Discuss answers with the whole group.

Session 7
Supporting your child – and you!

Materials needed
PowerPoint projector and screen
Handout 7

> **PowerPoint Slides 32–34**
>
> The aim of this session is to show how challenging behaviour can affect the family as a whole and what both parent and child need in order to deal with this.

Show PowerPoint Slide 32 to introduce the session. It may be useful to have a discussion, with those participants who are willing, about how the behaviour of their child has affected them. For example, they may have become selective about where they are willing to take them or there may be issues around schooling that means visiting the school frequently. Or there may be involvement with the authorities that places stress on home life, especially if one carer is dealing with more of the challenges than another, or if carers are inconsistent in their approach. Reinforce the need for consistency and for family members to work together as a team in order to address the issues being experienced.

Show PowerPoint Slide 33. Discuss the list of a child's needs and how these can be provided in the home environment. Explain that to enable children to manage their own behaviour parents need to provide an atmosphere of trust where they feel that they have the opportunity to participate in different activities and experiences.

Any situation can be a learning experience and children need to be encouraged to spread their wings and try different things, if they are ready to. If they are not ready they need to be reassured that this is OK and not made to feel unhappy by their inability to do something. Children should feel comfortable enough to talk and express themselves in their preferred way within the family, though parents should not feel that this must necessarily be with them. Some children find parents difficult to talk to but may find an older sibling or other family member or close friend easier to communicate with. It is also important that they have some time to themselves when they need it – we all feel the need to be on our own sometimes. Most importantly, parents need to help children find other ways to behave to replace the difficult behaviour. Remember that behaviour is an effective way for a child who has communication difficulties to make their needs known.

34 **Show PowerPoint Slide 34.** Ensure that the participants are aware that it is perfectly acceptable for them to have needs of their own and natural for them to experience a sense of helplessness because of their child's behaviour and their inability to understand and challenge those behaviours. Make sure they know that help is available from various sources. Emphasise that this training is about giving them the skills to cope. The chance to talk to other parents who are experiencing similar things is invaluable. Suggest that participants take the opportunity of sharing their problems with others they have met on the course. Often someone else has experienced the same or similar incidents and may be able to help by sharing information. It is also an opportunity to let off steam. When participants realise they are not alone they are more able to put things in perspective and this may lead to an increase in confidence in dealing with situations as they arise and an increase in their skills base. Explain that it is important that parents take time for themselves so that they can relax away from the day-to-day slog. It is not a bad thing for participants to want time for themselves and they should not feel guilty about it but accept the opportunity when it arises.

10 minutes

Distribute Handout 7 and ask participants to complete it. Discuss answers with the whole group.

10 minutes

Session 8
Summary

Materials needed
PowerPoint projector and screen
Handout 8
flipchart paper and pens

> **PowerPoint Slides 35–36**
> The aim of this session is to summarise the theory of why challenging behaviour occurs and what can be done to promote positive behaviour and reduce the likelihood of it occurring.

 Show PowerPoint Slide 35 to introduce the session.

 Show PowerPoint Slide 36 and run through the summary notes, stressing that there will still be difficult times. Explain that change does not come about overnight but only through persistence, perseverance and hard work. We may never know why a behaviour started but we can still manage and may be able to change it. Primarily, we want to reduce the impact on the child and family and to feel that we can achieve change.

Ask each participant to tell the group one or two things that they will take away with them that will help them and their child. Put these up on a flipchart to illustrate how much they have learned.

 Distribute Handout 8 and ask participants to complete it. Discuss answers with the whole group.

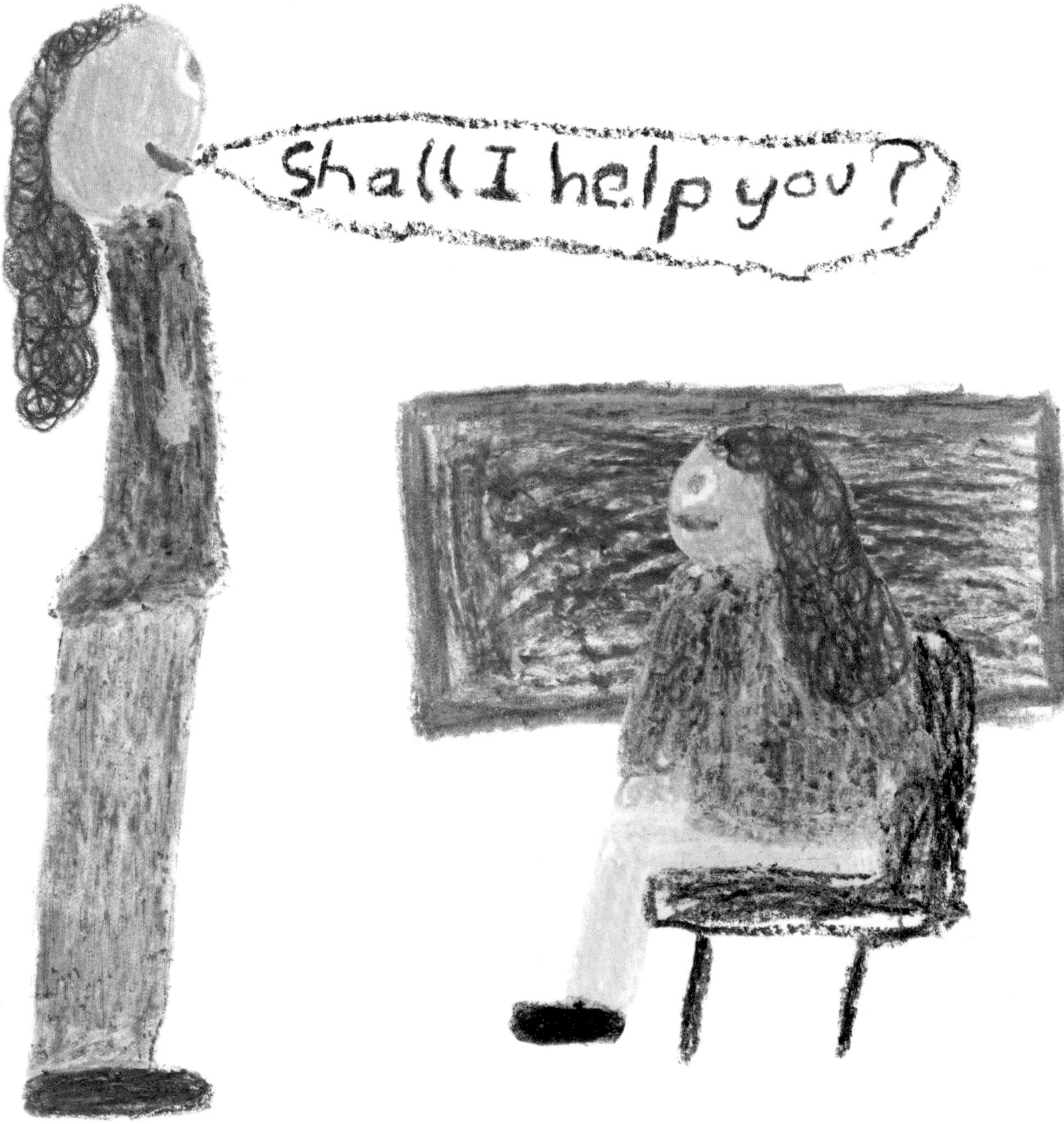
Shall I help you?